Yesterday's
—N°4—
Wirral
Wallasey and New Brighton
Including Leasowe

ABOVE Comic postcard from New Brighton

COVER New Brighton Tower 1905 (see page 16)

PRICE

By the same authors:-

YESTERDAY'S WIRRAL No 1 – Neston, Parkgate & Heswall

YESTERDAY'S WIRRAL No 2 – Birkenhead, Prenton & Oxton

YESTERDAY'S WIRRAL No 3 – West Kirby & Hoylake

Design – Colin McGuinness
Printed in Great Britain
          by Matthews Print Ltd., Liverpool
Typeset by Typebase Ltd
          1, Temple Court, Liverpool
Published by Ian & Marilyn Boumphrey

Introduction

The compilation of our fourth publication in a series concerned with various parts of the Wirral Peninsula has been particularly interesting. There has been a wealth of photographic material to draw upon, mainly in postcard form.

Mentioned in the Doomesday Book as Walea, which means the Island of Welshmen, the area was virtually isolated from the rest of Wirral by Wallasey Pool. This location formed a refuge for those seeking to avoid the invading Saxons. In later years the Wallasey coast gained a reputation for wrecking and smuggling. It was in 1830 that James Atherton, a retired Liverpool merchant, saw the opportunities that New Brighton offered with its extensive views, miles of golden sands and unique sights of ships in the Mersey. He developed the first villas and put New Brighton on the map as a resort. Initially it was the ferries which brought the visitors and later the railways, especially the Mersey Railway which opened in 1886. This also encouraged people working in Liverpool to live in the Wallasey area.

By the turn of the century, New Brighton had become more a popular resort than the exclusive residential and holiday area that James Atherton had envisaged, with the Tower leading the list of attractions. It was at this time that the residential areas of Wallasey grew and, helped by the electrification and extension of the tram routes from 1902, the country lanes which linked the townships of Wallasey became main roads. With the opening of the Mersey Tunnel in 1934 many more people came to live in the area, and New Brighton enticed the new trippers in cars by building a promenade with the largest outdoor swimming pool in the world.

New Brighton still flourished as a resort after the last war, but, with the coming of cheap holidays abroad, it lost its appeal. Many of its attractions disappeared, including the tower building, fairground, ferries and pier. However, the Floral Pavilion Theatre, open-air swimming pool, indoor fairground, ten-pin bowling alley, Aircraft Museum in the fort and other attractions are still popular, but the resort needs a face-lift to survive. Whether it will be the proposed Disney World type scheme that does it – only time will tell. Wallasey, as a residential area, is still a popular and pleasant place to live.

We hope you enjoy our choice of pictures, and that they will give you an insight into yesterday's Wallasey and perhaps bring back a few memories.

The rocks pictured behind the railings are known as the Red Noses. They form part of a sandstone ridge which extends parallel with the Mersey to Seacombe Point. It was here, in 1898, that evidence of a Neolithic settlement was found. The house on the right is now 50/54, Wellington Road. The building next door was demolished and in the late 1930's Portland Court was built on the site. This was the first major flats development in Wallasey, and was considered "decidedly American and a little daring"! Following the forming of the promenade in the 1930's the area in the foreground was built up, and the rocks have almost disappeared under the pitch & putt course. The Cliff Flats, which were built overlooking this site in 1964, cost one million pounds.

The Pembroke Chapel from Liverpool held an open-air service by the sea at New Brighton, near the Red Noses, on August Bank Holiday Sunday 1905. Upwards of seven thousand people gathered at seven o'clock to hear Rev. C.F. Aked preach. The collection taken was divided between Wallasey Central Hospital and Liverpool Sanitarium at Delamere Forest. This picture was taken a year later, in 1906, again on Bank Holiday Sunday, when Rev. Aked preached to upwards of ten thousand people. The peaceful surroundings, beautiful sunset and enormous congregation contributed to make the service a memorable one. New Brighton Tower can be seen in the background.

Taken in June 1934, this photograph shows the new Marine Promenade at New Brighton in front of the swimming pool *(see picture below)*. Work started in 1931 to extend the promenade from here to Harrison Drive. This was part of an ambitious scheme to encourage motorists and coaches using the new Mersey Tunnel, which was opened on 18 July 1934, to visit New Brighton. It included a massive concrete sea wall, a promenade 130 feet wide, a marine lake, an open-air bathing pool and envisaged 46 acres of public gardens. The line of the promenade was completed by 1939 but the war prevented the full development of the scheme which was never completed.

When New Brighton Swimming Pool was opened by Viscount Leverhulme on 13 June 1934 it was described as the largest bathing pool in the world. The picture above shows a queue forming for the new pool, which could accommodate up to ten thousand spectators and two thousand bathers. This photograph, with men in their one-piece costumes, shows how popular the baths were. Between June and September 1934 almost one million people went through the turnstiles. Fireworks were an added attraction, as was the Miss New Brighton competition which was started in 1949 and still continues. In 1984, the fiftieth year, Granada T.V. filmed a pop concert here and, although the high diving boards have gone, little has changed in fifty years.

Pictured is a small Houston liner, "The Fearless", which had collided with a coastal vessel on 6 February 1906 whilst proceeding from the Mersey to Hamburg with a cargo consisting mainly of fruit. She sustained a deep rent on the starboard side, resulting in the Captain beaching her on Egremont shore just north of the Mariners' Home. Gales played havoc with her during the following days, causing some of her cargo in crates and barrels to be seen floating in the Mersey. Part of the cargo was rescued by locals, who brought it ashore and surrendered it to the insurance company who paid one third of the price realised at auction. The vessel was eventually broken up on Trammere Foreshore.

It seems odd to us today that when this photograph was taken about 1908, three-piece suits, flat caps and bowlers were the fashion for the seaside. New Brighton Lighthouse was erected on the sandstone outcrop of Perch Rock. Built for Liverpool Dock Trustees and based on the design of Eddystone Lighthouse, the foundation stone was laid on 8 June 1827. Granite was brought from Anglesey and volcanic cement from the slopes of Mount Etna. The ninety foot high building was opened on 1 March 1830. The lighthouse was sold off in the 1970's and has been refurbished. It is now let out particularly to honeymoon couples looking for an unusual venue for their wedding night.

THE BATTERY, NEW BRIGHTON.   No 3214.

In 1803, during the Napoleonic wars, it was decided by leading Liverpool dignitaries and merchants that a battery should be erected at the mouth of the river on Perch Rock and another on the Lancashire side. However, due to disagreements, work was not started on Fort Perch Rock until 31 March 1826, and was completed on 30 April 1829 at a cost of £26,965. Built of Runcorn Sandstone, to the design of Captain J.S. Kitson of the Royal Engineers, with accommodation for over 100 men, the defence included 18 guns. Improvements were made from 1861 onwards, providing stronger defences and better guns. *(see below)*.

THE BATTERY, SHOWING TOWER, NEW BRIGHTON.

Fort Perch Rock is seen from the river about 1914, and compares with the 1932 view above taken from the promenade. In March 1893 the battery was dismantled and the building taken over in 1894 by the Royal Engineers who lowered parts of the walls to the rear of the fort by eleven feet. This enabled the three new 6 inch guns, which became operational in March 1899, to hit targets as near as 150 yards. These guns were replaced in 1910 by the three Mark VII 6 inch guns pictured, of which two were sent for duty elsewhere in 1916, one being returned in 1923. The guns were last fired during the Festival of Britain in 1951 and were dismantled in 1954. The fort is now open to the public, and includes a unique collection of World War Two aircraft relics.

This Manx steamer, "King Orry", left Douglas at 9 a.m. on 19 August 1921, carrying a full complement of passengers bound for Liverpool. Due to thick fog in the Mersey it became stranded in firm sand just a few yards from Perch Rock at New Brighton. At low tide crowds were able to walk round her and carry on conversations with the passengers. The Wallasey Fire Brigade rendered useful service to the stranded passengers by placing their fire escape against the side of the ship to enable them to leave the vessel. Later that night, at high tide, the ship was towed to safety and was back in service within four days.

This picture, with New Brighton Tower in the background, shows members of Liverpool City Mission holding a well-attended service on the shore, which, until the new promenade was built in 1907, came right up to the wall of Marine Parade. The services included singing, for which musical accompaniment was provided by the lady seated to the right of the gentleman at the centre of the group. Behind the railings is Marine Park which was opened in 1897 and boasted a fine bandstand where concerts were performed twice weekly. Rowson Street, where most of the premises were refreshment or dining rooms, lies beyond the park.

Although most of the buildings in this turn of the century photograph are still standing today, the scene has changed dramatically *(see below)*. The area of sand pictured in front of the hotels was developed into the present Marine Promenade, starting in 1907. The bottom of Rowson Street is behind the donkey stand on the right, with New Brighton Tower in the background. Waterloo Road extended as far as the building on the left, which is a steakhouse today. The far building of those in the long row is the Queen's Royal Hotel, and next door, with the wrought iron balcony, is the Marine Hotel where pierrots performed from a stage fronting onto the sands.

This Edwardian scene of 1910 is photographed from a similar position to the one above. It shows what a complete physical change the new promenade made to New Brighton, bringing it a new respectability. The planner showed much foresight in building the road so wide, especially as there was very little traffic on the roads at that time. The only wheels in sight are on the pram, and the children's roller skates. A group of Edwardian ladies and gentlemen are seen taking a stroll along the promenade, black being the fashionable colour.

The Palace, pictured in 1907 when the Council purchased the property for £41,500, dates back to 1880. Salt water baths were opened here in 1881 and four years later, at a cost of 6d, entertainments included:- the finest ballroom in England, skating rink, aviary, grotto and two concert halls. By 1889 it had the largest plunge baths in the country and in 1896 the new owners planned building the largest Big Wheel in the world, similar to one at Earl's Court, but this never happened. All the buildings to the left of The Palace were demolished after work started on the new promenade in 1907, and were replaced by Victoria Gardens *(see opposite)*. The New Palace, with indoor amusements, now occupies the site of The Palace.

Originally built around 1871, the single storied Lower Parade with the Higher Parade above, are seen on the left. The Lower Parade was better known as the infamous Ham & Egg Parade, which was to give New Brighton a bad name. This reputation came from the many refreshment and dining room proprietors who would accost passers-by to entice them into their premises. In 1905 the Lower Parade was so busy that women and children were pushed off the unfenced causeway onto the sands. On 27 January 1906 a local referendum voted for the Council to purchase and demolish the Ham & Egg Parade buildings and extend the promendade to Waterloo Road. Work started in 1907, and the Victoria Gardens, which replaced the parade, were opened on 3 May 1913.

The Victoria Gardens are pictured here shortly after they were opened by Lord Derby on 3 May 1913, on the site once occupied by the infamous Ham & Egg Parade *(see page 10)*. By ridding itself of this embarrassing eyesore and replacing it with gardens and a theatre, New Brighton was hoping to attract back some of its lost visitors. There were not sufficient funds to build a covered theatre initially but the open-air Summer Theatre, in the centre of the picture, proved very popular in good weather. In 1925 a glass structure enclosed the theatre and it then became known as The Floral Pavilion *(see below)*.

The open-air theatre pictured above was covered in and named The Floral Pavilion in 1925. This meant that shows were no longer dependant on the weather. The Optimists were appearing when this 1920's photograph was taken, and the seats were priced at 4d, 6d and 1/2d. Pierrot and concert shows were popular until the 1940's. In 1948 Jackson Earle introduced the first "Melody Inn Review". These were to run for a record-breaking 25 years. The glass structure was replaced at a cost of £55,000, re-opening in May 1965 as The Floral Pavilion Theatre. The past decade has seen a host of stars appearing on the stage as well as local amateur productions.

This wooden pier was built in the 1830's by William Rowson to improve the ferry embarkation point to Liverpool. One of the early boats was the old "Liverpool", a paddle steamer built in 1830 and described thus – "An awful old tub with cog wheels inside which rattled so much you could not hear yourself speak". The journey to Liverpool normally took half an hour, but when the weather was very bad it took a whole day to make the trip. This Heath-Robinson affair must have been more substantial than it looked, lasting more than thirty years. New Brighton Ferry was purchased by Mr. E.W. Coulbourn in 1850 and, in 1860, it passed into the hands of the Local Board; the pier being rebuilt in iron 1865-7.

The first column of this pier was fixed in place on 19 December 1866 and the pier was opened in September 1867, replacing the old wooden structure pictured above. The pier on the left, which was then privately owned and where admission when this picture was taken in 1914 was 3d, was for entertainment only. One of the billboards advises that the Birkenhead Corporation Band was appearing at the Pier Pavilion, whilst the banner above the pier entrance advertises the Great Cycle Dive. This trick was performed by Prof. J.O. Matchett, who came from Liverpool. He travelled the resorts of Great Britain, Ireland and parts of the U.S.A. giving his displays. The pier on the right was for passengers using the New Brighton Ferry *(see next page)*.

The bank holiday scene shows how popular New Brighton was in 1914, when the majority of men wore either boaters or flat caps, whilst the ladies are seen in attractive hats. Most of these trippers were from Liverpool or other Lancashire industrial towns, and had crossed the Mersey for the day to enjoy the sea air, golden sands and the excitement New Brighton had to offer. The Council purchased the pier in 1928 when it had been condemned by the Board of Trade. However, following repairs and the addition of a lounge, a clubhouse for the West Cheshire Sailing Club and a large bandstand, it re-opened in 1931, remaining virtually unaltered until it was demolished in July 1978.

The floating landing stage was connected to the pier by two bridges. Erected in 1867, it was renewed in 1921 and finally closed in 1972. The "J. Farley" pictured was delivered in 1922 together with her sister ship "Francis Storey", named respectively after the chairman and former chairman of the Ferries Committee. They were used on the Seacombe route until 1928, when they were transferred to New Brighton. They were commandeered by the Admiralty in 1942/43 when, manned by Wallasey Ferry crews, they became net carriers, installing anti-torpedo nets on merchant ships. They returned to ferry duties in 1946 and operated until "Francis Storey" was sold in 1951 and "J. Farley" in 1952.

Royal Daffodil in War-Time

The "Daffodil", shown here and her sister ship "Iris" entered the ferry service in July 1906. They were a great improvement on previous boats and served New Brighton in its hey-day. In April 1918 both boats were armour-plated and sent as troop carriers in the raid on Zeebrugge to block the port for enemy submarines. Under heavy fire and making smoke screens they withdrew after the gallant raid. The "Daffodil" returned in tow and "Iris" under her own steam. After extensive refits they returned to ferry duties in 1919 with the prefix "Royal" in recognition of their heroic deed. In 1923 the "Royal Iris" was used for Summer excursions and when she was sold in 1931 the "Royal Daffodil" succeeded her until she too was sold in 1933.

THE PIER AND SANDS, NEW BRIGHTON

This picture was taken on New Brighton sands, with the pier in the background, in 1911. Behind the families walking on the sands are female hawkers from Liverpool, most of whom are seated. Some sixty of these hawkers would cross the Mersey daily in the summer with their large wicker baskets. Their wares included New Brighton rock, coloured drinks, paper windmills, strings of shells and beads, postcards, etc. Some Italian girls even sold cages of love-birds. The New Brighton shopkeepers made bitter complaints to the Council about these ladies as they were taking away their trade. Many of the hawkers received fines of 2/6d and 5/–, but this did not deter them as they all clubbed together to pay the fines.

The "Horse Shoe" is the area pictured at the bottom of Victoria Road in front of the pier. The ornamental lamp stands in the centre of the terminus for the electric tram routes to New Brighton, the first of which ran from Seacombe Ferry, opening on 17 March 1902. The covered-in tram No.29 operated on the Warren Drive route, and awaits its passengers off the ferry. In 1910 the Royal Ferry Hotel, pictured on the right, advertised that it had been frequented by Charles Dickens in the 1860's. A brass plaque was erected above the seat that he was said to have used, and this created great interest. However, it was later found to be a hoax to boost trade!

PHOTO: R. EASTHAM]   NEW BRIGHTON LIFEBOATMEN.

This picture postcard of the New Brighton lifeboatmen was bought at a dramatic performance given in aid of their funds at the New Brighton Assembly Rooms in Albion Street *(see page 18)* in February 1910. In July of that year the fifteenth Annual New Brighton Lifeboat Day was held. Copies of this postcard were sent to local tradesmen who had businesses on the processional route, asking them to decorate their premises. The Birkenhead Borough Silver Prize Band led the parade from Vernon's Fields in Birkenhead Road, Seacombe via Liscard to New Brighton sands where sports were held. These included climbing the greasy pole, a treacle bun eating competition, tug-of-war and a sack race. Street collecting boxes raised £140 for the lifeboat fund.

The erection of New Brighton Tower, which was once considered the eighth wonder of the world, commenced in June 1896. The grounds opened at Whitsun 1897 and the Tower in 1900. At 621 feet above sea-level it was the tallest structure in England. On a clear day the Isle of Man could be seen from the viewing platform, as could Blackpool Tower which was some 100 feet shorter. Sixpence gained entry to the 35 acres of grounds and covered entry to most of the attractions, which included beautiful gardens, a lake with gondolas and genuine gondoliers, a fairground, water-chute, Himalayan Railway, the Tower Theatre which seated 3,000 with a stage which could accommodate a whole circus, a ballroom, billiard saloon, monkey house and aviary.

NEW BRIGHTON *from the Air.*

This aerial view of the partly demolished Tower shows the oval athletics arena which stood within its grounds. Opening in 1897, the grounds featured a cycle-track where the 1922 World Championships were held, and a running track; later the centre area became the home of New Brighton Football Club. The Tower was at the height of its popularity during the Edwardian Era. On Whit Monday 1910, when the main attraction was a balloon ascent, there were over 51,000 visitors. Due to lack of maintenance during the war years the 1,000 ton steel structure became unsafe and the Tower was dismantled between May 1919 and June 1920. It was during this time that the picture was taken.

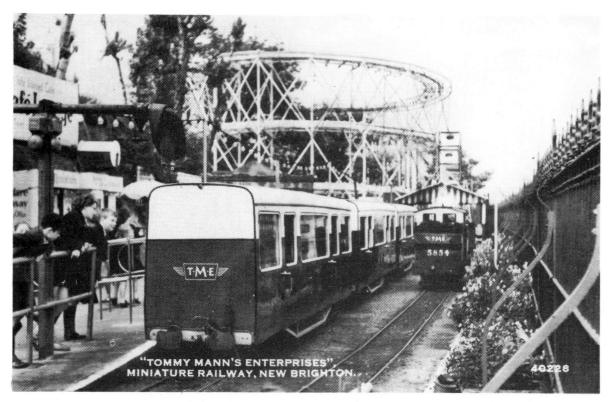

"TOMMY MANN'S ENTERPRISES",
MINIATURE RAILWAY, NEW BRIGHTON.
40228

Even without its top, the Tower building and grounds still provided plenty of entertainment between the wars. It was described in a 1931 holiday guide as the "largest permanent pleasure resort in the U.K.", boasting of the largest ballroom in the North of England which could accommodate up to a thousand dancers, a theatre and a waxworks. Outside, the attractions included side-shows, a boating lake, a figure-of-eight and a joy-wheel. The entertainment continued after the Second World War and visitors from the late 1940's to the 1960's were able to enjoy the varied amusements provided by the New Brighton Tower Company. "Tommy Mann's Enterprises" miniature railway is pictured in the 1960's with the figure-of-eight in the background.

This aerial view taken on a Bank Holiday in 1960, when the Tower was described as the "playground of the North", shows how popular New Brighton still was. This was the year in which the chair-lift first operated from near the promenade to the roof of the Tower building. Other attractions advertised for that year included a zoo, skating, waxworks, and a boating lake. Many stars appeared at the ballroom, including The Beatles and Gerry and The Pacemakers on 14 June 1963. The Tower building was damaged by fire on 5 April 1969, and was later demolished. After many years of indecision over their future, the grounds were eventually developed and houses now occupy the site.

The Convalescent Home for Women and Children, pictured here about 1906 in Rowson Street, New Brighton, was established in 1847. The former nursing home was acquired in 1924 by the Sisters of the Holy Family, and Maris Stella Convent was formed. The sisters had opened a convent and school in a large house in Wellington Road, which was retained as a mixed preparatory school when the senior girls moved to the newly acquired premises in Rowson Street. This was the first Roman Catholic High School in the town, and at one time had 500 pupils. As a result of the changing pattern of education in the district both schools closed in 1972. The high school was demolished in 1973 and flats now occupy the site.

Victoria Hotel, with its magnificent views over the River Mersey, provided accommodation for some of the first visitors to New Brighton. Opened in the 1830's it was run by John Garrett and was later known as the Hotel Victoria as seen in this advertising card circa 1910. By the 1920's telegrams were to be directed to "COMFORT – WALLASEY". During World War II an air raid shelter was constructed under the hotel. In the adjoining Assembly Rooms in Albion Street, Mrs Pankhurst addressed an audience in October 1910 on the subject of the suffragette movement. It was here, three years earlier in the summer of 1907, that a small, mild, bespectacled man gave a medical lecture. He was to gain world renown a few years later as the murderer Dr. Crippen.

An Edwardian photograph has captured this scene looking down Victoria Road at its junction with Rowson Street. The open-topped tram in the middle distance operated on lines in the centre of the road and is seen passing horses and carts on either side of the road. As it operated on the Seabank Road route, which opened on 19 March 1902, it would take the track to the right up Rowson Street, then along Seabank Road to Seacombe Ferry. In the summer of 1931 Victoria Road was used as an experimental one-way street but, due to opposition from local shopkeepers whose takings were down, the idea was abandoned. The North and South Wales Bank on the left is now the Midland Bank.

Rowson Street, with Molyneux Drive on the right, is pictured in 1915. The letter 'S' on the covered-in trams denotes that they operated on the Seabank Road route. On the right is the Sandrock Hotel. In the early days of summer visitors, accomodation was found on arrival and touts would extol the virtues of various boarding houses, offering apartments for 1/6d per day. Landladies would often cook meals with food provided by the guests. Many of the smaller hotels had no electricity and musical evenings were popular. The Sandrock Hotel, which was occupied by American servicemen from 1942-1945, closed down about 1979. Since 1981 it has been occupied by Wilson & Southern, Auctioneers.

The buildings seen in this c1911 view of Rowson Street have not changed much in 75 years. The Little Brighton Inn, pictured on the right, is not mentioned as a licensed premises in 1850 but by 1860 John Evans was the proprietor. The Sandridge, on the opposite side of the road, is also there today. The tram lines, which swept round to the left and into Rake Lane, formed the first electric tram route, opened on 17 March 1902. Behind the wall on the left is the Quarry Pleasure Ground, still used by bowlers today. The gap in the wall in front of the hand-cart has been filled in, and access to the park is by the Clock Memorial entrance, which was erected in memory of Councillor James Smith 1841-1909.

St. James', the Parish Church of New Brighton, is pictured here in Victoria Road in 1908. The foundation stone was laid by the Bishop of Chester on 16 February 1854, but damage, due to gales and storms, delayed the consecration until 10 July 1856. Built in the Gothic Style, the church was originally lit by oil lamps until 1860 when gas lamps were installed and finally connected to electricity in 1900. Being in an exposed position, the church has been repaired many times due to the weather, it also suffered slight bomb damage in the last war. Fowell Road, between the church and the house on the right, was named after the first vicar.

"Sandrock" pictured here, was built in 1845 and stood at the top of St. Georges Mount at its junction with Atherton Street. In May 1911 it was bought by a French Roman Catholic Order known as The Sisters of the Cenacle who converted it into a nunnery. During the Great War it became a Red Cross Hospital, treating more than 700 wounded soldiers. The nuns moved to a new building in Wavertree and, in the mid-1920's, the then derelict house was bought for the Church of SS Peter & Paul under the guidance of Father Mullins. About ten years later a new church was built on the site (see below).

The Roman Catholic Church of SS Peter & Paul had its beginnings in 1879 in a rented room in Egerton Street. It was not until June 1881 that a Gothic style church was erected in Hope Street at its junction with Rowson Street. In July 1885 a school opened opposite the church with just 70 pupils. When Father Mullins became Rector in 1909 he established a fund for a new church. The foundation stone was laid on the site of "Sandrock" on 30 July 1932, and the first Mass celebrated in August 1935. The church, which seats 650, cost £58,000. A new primary school was opened in January 1951 on a site to the right of the photograph. The Monti Bello Hotel, pictured in the background, was demolished after World War II.

This half-timbered Victorian building once stood on Egremont Promenade between Lincoln Drive and Caithness Drive, and was known as Mother Redcap's. The original building which was erected in 1595 and rebuilt in 1888 became a tavern in the early eighteenth century and was noted for its strong home-brewed ale. It was not until the late eighteenth century that the inn was run by a lady, who always wore a red cap, and hence gave the inn its name. She was a trusted friend to all seafarers, and legends abound of wreckers and smugglers, excise men and press gangs, hidden doors and secret passages, smugglers' caves and buried treasure. The Victorian building was demolished in October 1974 and flats were to be built on the land. The site however remains empty.

This view of the Liverpool Home for Aged Mariners is taken from Egremont Promenade. Built on a five acre site, fronting onto Seabank Road at its junction with Maddock Road, it offered the retired seaman a commanding view of the Mersey. William Cliff built the home in memory of his daughter, Rosa Webster, from plans by Col. David Walker and it was opened on 16 December 1882 by the Duke of Edinburgh. The main building, which housed the single men, was surmounted by a tower 135 feet high, with a fine clock and bell. Numerous cottages were built in the grounds to house the married men. The bunting was probably to celebrate the visit of King George V to lay the foundation stone of the Town Hall.

Looking from Egremont Ferry, this was the second section of promenade to be constructed. Prior to this the river frontage was largely open to the shore. Started in 1891 it was forty-five feet wide and continued as far as Holland Road. This photograph was probably taken between 1891 and 1899 when work commenced on the stretch of promenade from Holland Road to beyond New Brighton Pier, which can be seen in the right background. Also, New Brighton Tower, the grounds of which were opened in 1897, was not built when this photograph was taken. The tower in the centre belongs to the Mariners' Home *(see previous picture)*.

This unusual view of the frozen Mersey at Egremont Pier was taken in February 1895. Large ice-floes had come down from the upper reaches of the river, bringing small ice-bergs and at low tide the Mersey had the appearance of a vast ice field. The river remained like this for a few weeks before the thaw set in. Egremont Ferry was acquired c1830 by Capt. John Askew, Harbour Master of Liverpool, who named it after his native town in Cumberland. The ferry and boats were bought by the Local Board in 1862. A new iron pier and landing stage were constructed for £14,000 and opened on 25 March 1875. The pier was finally put out of commission in 1941, after being rammed and was dismantled in 1946.

This mid-twenties aerial view of Seacombe Ferry, shows the buildings opened in January 1880 which were constructed when the land was reclaimed in 1876. The Seacombe Ferry Hotel, pictured to the left of the ferry, was opened about the same time replacing previous hotels which had existed behind the old high-water mark since at least the seventeenth century. The hotel was well-known for its catering, appearing in the Good Food Guide in the 1960's. It was demolished in 1978 and replaced by a smaller hotel at a cost of £150,000. A ferry-boat can be seen at the landing stage, with a luggage boat to the right. The war-damaged funnel of the Royal Iris can be seen at the waters edge, south of the ferry premises.

On 12 February 1909 the Dominion liner "Ottoman" tried to avoid several Liverpool flats and a Pacific liner off Seacombe. In so doing "Ottoman" headed towards the landing stage. Realising a collision was inevitable, orders were given to drop the anchor, and fenders were then lowered over the side to cushion the impact which was terrific. The gangways on the north end were almost smashed to pieces. The platform and hydraulic rams sustained severe damage and passengers had to be landed by the other gangways. This was one of many accidents involving the Wallasey Ferries over the years due to the close proximity of Liverpool's shipping.

Victoria Place, Seacombe about 1904 depicts the bustle of Edwardian life. The nearest tram is off to New Brighton via Rake Lane, whilst two other trams await customers off the ferry. For the passenger who required a more personal service, hackney cabs are available in the centre of the roadway. The ladies in their long dresses hold on to their hats, whilst two paper boys on the left pose for the photographer. The ferry buildings date back to 1880 *(see opposite)*, when the first floating landing stage was built. This was replaced in 1926 by a new landing stage and three-track floating roadway, which cost £204,000. Difficulties arose in dealing with the increased traffic, so work started on a new terminus building in 1930.

Taken in 1932, this photograph of the Seacombe Ferry buildings was taken after the clock tower and right side of the new building had been completed *(see above)*. Three types of transport vie for the passengers' custom:- the motor-cabs on the left have replaced the horse-drawn ones, the trams on the right were eventually phased out, the last tramcar running on 30 November 1933; and the buses which first operated from here to Harrison Drive on 3 April 1920. The buildings were fully opened on 10 April 1933. The ferry buildings were chosen by E.M.I. in 1984 as a setting for their film "Dream Child", based on an Alice in Wonderland theme.

Liscard Battery which was near the site of the former Magazines, is pictured here in 1905, taken from Fort Street with Magazine Brow on the right. The family on the left is walking down Magazine Lane to Egremont Promenade. The Magazines were transferred here from Liverpool and were in use by 1768. Ships entering the Mersey had to deposit any gunpowder here during their stay in port. In 1851 an Act of Parliament effected their removal to vessels anchored off New Ferry, much to the relief of local residents. The Battery, built of red sandstone in 1858, was armed with guns and provided accommodation for regular soldiers. By October 1912 it had become obsolete and was sold to Liverpool Yacht Club for £1,600.

Both the Magazine Hotel pictured on the left, and Magazine Brow, the road in which it stands, derive their names from their proximity to the Liscard Magazines *(see previous picture)*. All were built about the same time as the hotel, which has a date stone RT 1759. As the original one acre site for the magazines was chosen for its remoteness, the hotel must have been one of the few buildings in the area at that time. Most of the trade came from sailors waiting for gunpowder to be loaded or unloaded from their ships. Another old building that survives is the Round House in Fort Street, where the watchmen from the magazines lived. The building on the left was a boot and shoe makers shop.

This tram is proceeding along King Street towards Seacombe Ferry in 1905. The Egremont United Presbyterian Church is pictured on the right at the junction with Trafalgar Road. The foundation stone was laid on 2 December 1862, and the cost of building was about £4,000. The church moved to a new site in Seabank Road at its junction with Manor Road, and was consecrated on 1 October 1908. The former church opened as a cinema in January 1910, and operated until 30 December 1931 when fire destroyed the building. The Gaumont Palace opened here on 13 November 1933 and continued until Unit Four Cinemas took over in October 1974. The building on the left now houses the block of shops which includes the sub-post office.

This elephant, which probably came from New Brighton Tower Zoo, must have been an odd sight in the streets of Egremont where it was advertising the Royal Cinedrome which was on the site of the former Volunteer Drill Shed in King Street built in or about 1864. The Royal Cinedrome opened on 4 November 1912. The building which had been the home of the Third Cheshire Rifles, was later a skating rink and, in June 1929, became the first cinema in Wallasey to show talking pictures. In 1948 the cinema was bought by Mr. Wilkie, proprietor of New Brighton Amusement Park. The cinema closed on 28 January 1967 when it became a bingo hall, and is currently in use as a snooker hall.

The photographer was standing at the junction of four roads when he took this picture in 1904. King Street is ahead, Tobin Street, which led to Egremont Ferry, is on the right, Brighton Street is behind him, and the policeman on the left stands at the entrance to Church Street. It was in Church Street that Wallasey Town Hall functioned from 1854 until it moved to the Brighton Street premises in 1920. Mackie & Gladstone's premises are pictured behind the policeman, where a dozen bottles of Guinness could be purchased for three shillings. The buildings on the left have made way for a block of flats and shops. The North and South Wales Bank on the right is now the Old Bank pub.

Looking down River View Road, Seacombe, Brougham Road is on the left and Guinea Gap Baths, which were opened in 1908, are on the right. Since 1900 the question of the siting of the new Town Hall, pictured centre, had been a controversial one. However, the foundation stone was laid by King George V on 25 March 1914 in Brighton Street. The authorities gave up possession to the War Office and from early 1916 the building was adapted as a military hospital. By 1919, when the hospital closed, 3,500 wounded soldiers had been treated in the makeshift wards. The Town Hall was officially opened on 3 November 1920 by the then Mayor of Wallasey, Alderman E.G. Parkinson.

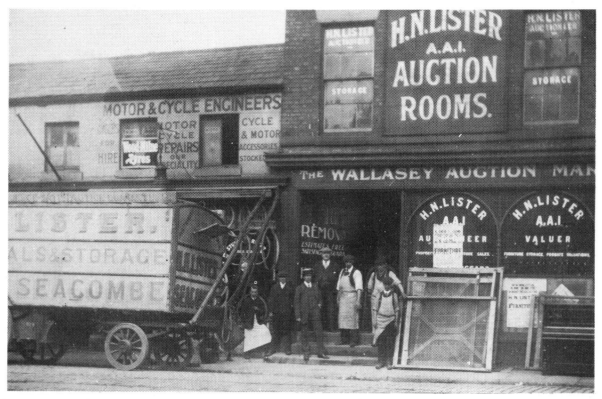

Henry Northing Lister is pictured here with some of his employees outside his auction rooms at No. 4 Desmesne Street, Seacombe. He also operated weekly auctions from his rooms at 107, Seaview Road, Liscard and 110, Chester Street, Birkenhead. Pictured on the left is one of his removal wagons with wooden shafts for the shire horse and the driver's seat can be seen high up at the front. Lister only operated for a few years before the First World War and, by 1915, the building was occupied by a wardrobe dealer. Behind the wagon are the premises of Rumph & Davies who were motor and cycle engineers, that stood on the corner of Brougham Road, just along the road to the right of the previous picture.

This 1904 picture was taken by Arthur Shaw of Seacombe who also photographed the one opposite. Taken in the centre of Victoria Road (now Borough Road) Brighton Street is ahead and Church Road behind the photographer. A flat-hatted policeman stands under the ornate lamp on the left, whilst the gentleman on the right waits in front of Burrows, manufacturers and dealers in boots and shoes. In 1906 they held a sale of gents' shoes priced from 3/10d to 18/–, and ladies' boots priced from 2/11d to 12/6d. Next door at No. 2, Cambrian Buildings, Brighton Street is a grocer and provision dealer's shop with a hand-cart outside. A flour dealer and baker named Lacy had premises on the corner of Little Street. Borough Way now occupies the site.

This 1907 view of St. Paul's Church, which stands at the head of the approach from Seacombe Ferry, was taken from St. Paul's Road. The foundation stone was laid on 6 June 1846, and the church was consecrated on 12 October 1847. Built in the style of the thirteenth century, its 120 foot spire was completed in 1849. Electric lighting was introduced in 1906, as were the marble altar steps. In the 1920's the top of the spire became twisted and unsafe, but was not removed until 1975. The spire is at present being re-pointed. The buildings on the right are St. Paul's School in Bridle Road *(see below);* Seacombe Ferry buildings are in the distance.

This photograph of Dehany Bros. Cycle and Motor Engineers of Bridle Road, Seacombe, was taken about 1914, the year they took over this site from a builder. The car is a 1913 Prince Henry Vauxhall with Mr. J.E. Dehany Snr. on the left, Sandy Baines, and Jim Dehany Jnr. on the right. The yard was extended just after the First World War. The Dehanys, who had gained a reputation as one of the best motor engineering firms in the area, sold the business in September 1967. The building is still occupied by motor engineers. St. Paul's School on the right became the church hall in 1933. About 1970 the auctioneers, Wilson & Southern, operated from this building which was demolished in 1982 and the site acquired for sheltered housing.

This small wooden structure in Church Road, Seacombe, was the first premises of Russell & Robinson who opened their wholesale newsagents business here in 1921. Theirs was a spectacular growth for, three years later, Russell Buildings were constructed across the road. The datestone of 1924 can still be seen above the present D.I.Y. Store. Russell & Robinson built the single-storied building next door which was later taken over by W.H. Smith and is now St. Paul's Church Hall. When Russell & Robinson moved into their new premises the building pictured here became a pet store which was well known for its monkeys on chains and parrots. The local police station was on the left. A block of flats now occupies the site.

This group of railway dignitaries, which includes third from left Tom Williams, the great-grandfather of the authoress, is pictured on Seacombe and Egremont platform just prior to the First World War. As far back as 1863 Parliamentary permission had been granted to connect Hoylake and Seacombe by rail. However, mainly due to the high cost of building cuttings and fourteen over-bridges, the line was not opened until 1 June 1895. This was originally intended as a temporary station. It was planned to extend the line a further 140 yards where the railway and ferry terminal were to be built side-by-side. This proposal was never carried out. The station closed to passengers on 3 January 1960 and to goods on 17 June 1963. Flats now occupy the station site.

The employees of Jones & Williams, 1a, Brighton Street, Seacombe are seen here displaying some of their wrought ironwork. The company's delivery horse and cart can be seen on the left; the buildings in the background are the rear of houses in Victoria Street (now Borough Road). An advertisement in a Wallasey Gazette of 1914 states:- "Jones & Williams, Victoria Iron Works, Seacombe – Manufacturers of iron gates, railings, plain and ornamental builders' ironwork, wheelrights forge for shoeing (behind N & S Wales Bank, Victoria Street)". The business which continued as Jones & Williams later became blacksmiths' and builders' plumbers' merchants. They closed in the 1950's and the building is now used for car repairs and servicing.

The sight of these carcases, which are seen hanging outside J.H. Scott's premises about 1920, would be considered unhygenic today, but was commonplace then. Standing on the corner of Church Road and Victoria Road (now Borough Road) this family butcher was also a shipping purveyor, using his slaughterhouse on the premises. The sign on the centre carcase states that this prime bullock was bred and fed by C. Lee of Chester. Founded in the 1890's, this business continued until between the wars when the premises were taken over by the Prudential Assurance Company who removed the signboards and miniature bulls' heads replacing them with their own name which is still there today although the building is now unoccupied.

The photographer took this 1904 picture, which looks right up Victoria Road (now Borough Road), whilst standing outside Scott's shop shown in the previous picture. Adults and children alike pose for the photographer, with the exception of the window cleaner on the left behind Brick's sign, who carried on regardless. Brick, who was a boot and shoe manufacturer and repairer, was also a receiving officer for goods and parcels for the L & N.W. Railway Company. This block of shops still stands today. Opposite, and out of the picture on the corner of Brighton Street, was the North and South Wales Bank which opened in February 1895. This later became a branch of the Midland Bank. The girl on the right, holding onto her hat, stands in front of J. Robinsons Tinsmiths shop.

Taken at the same time as the previous picture but from the opposite end of Victoria Road, one can see what a busy area this was. The fruiterer and florist poses in front of her wares on the right, whilst next door the barber waits for customers attracted by his large advertising board which states:- "U – NEED – A – SHAVE, step right in". Florence Road is behind the crowd on the right. Bell's stores opened the new branch at 99, Victoria Road, Seacombe in February 1906, and some of the introductory offers included:- lean picnic hams at 4½d per pound; finest dairy butter at 1/– per pound; and a good pair of corsets given free with two pounds of tea!

Brougham House, pictured here in the 1890's, once stood on the corner of Liscard Road and Brougham Road. This 2,150 square yard site was purchased by the Seacombe Presbyterian Church for £1,550 in August 1906. The church was founded back in December 1862 in a disused Wesleyan Chapel in Wheatland Lane. The chapel was repaired and used until the new Mission House in Church Road, Seacombe, was dedicated on 20 July 1869. The total cost was £2,496, with the main hall being used as a schoolroom on weekdays, and as a church on Sundays. An extension, called Western Hall, opened in 1879 at a cost of £958, but when church membership began to show a rapid increase some four years later, the Mission House was proved too small *(see next picture)*.

Following the purchase of Brougham House in 1906 *(see above),* there were insufficient funds to build a new church on the site. Money raising events were held, including bazaars, concerts and sales of work. Also 134 square yards of the land were sold to the Council. In 1909 a bazaar guide was produced which gave the membership as 204 and Sunday scholars 411. On 29 July 1911 the foundation stone was laid and the new church of Gothic design, pictured here about 1950, was dedicated on 25 September 1912. The Mission House in Church Road was closed and eventually sold to Wallasey Printers. The new halls, to the right of the church, were opened 23 January 1926. The church, which survived the Second World War with minor damage, still thrives today.

The weather must have been fine in Liscard Road when this photograph was taken in the early 1900's, as passengers are enjoying the ride on the top of this No. 22 tram. Martins Lane is in front of the houses on the right and in the background to the left of the tram is Victoria Central Hospital. Named after Queen Victoria, the foundation stone was laid on 6 July 1899, opening on 1 January 1901 with 36 beds and 6 cots. The hospital served Wallasey well until May 1982 when the new Arrowe Park Hospital was opened, centralising Wirral's medical services. The site is now occupied by an ambulance station and the Liscard Nursing & Residential Home, which was opened by Lynda Chalker M.P. on 7 March 1986.

Taken from Serpentine Road, Liscard, Martins Lane follows the road to the left in front of the ivy-covered building, which is on the corner of Withens Lane. First mentioned in a Directory of 1860, when George Evanson was the victualler of the Primrose Tavern, the building later became the Primrose Hotel. The hotel, which was structurally altered in 1923, was famous for its rose gardens which survived until the present car park replaced them a few years ago. The building to the right comprised Nos 96 & 98, Greenwood Lane. When Withens Lane was widened the left half of the building was demolished and the remaining half converted into shops.

Withens Lane pictured in the 1920's was described in 1910 as one of the few remaining old and narrow lanes in the district and was widened at a cost of £203. The wagon is delivering to Bents wine store at No. 20. This is still an off-licence, and Bents Ale & Stout advertisement can still be seen on the door. The van in the distance is calling at the Saddle Inn which was originally two cottages built in the 1830's and became an inn about 1888. St. Mary's, Liscard Parish Church, which was consecrated on 13 December 1877, is in the background. The large house in front of the church, on the corner of Manor Road, has been demolished and flats now occupy the site.

Pictured here with broken windows and in need of repair is Liscard Castle, or Marsden's Folly, shortly before it was demolished about 1902. Note the stone lion guarding the castle from the top battlements. At one time the castle was occupied by Mr. John Astley Marsden, who was a manufacturer of brushes in Liverpool, and it became known locally as Brush Castle. This building stood at the Hose Side Road end of Seaview Road; Castle Road and Turret Road now mark the site. John Marsden was a principal landowner and it was he who had the Liscard Congregational Church built in Rake Lane at a cost of £1,200. The church opened 1 September 1842.

Wallasey Grammar School buildings are pictured here in Withens Lane. There are few records of the early history of the school, but the death of a schoolmaster in 1595 is on record. The first school was probably under the same roof as the parish church, until it moved to new premises in Breck Road in 1799 *(see page 48)*. An increase in population led to the school moving to St. Georges Road in 1864 and, twelve years later, to Withens Lane, where the new buildings, pictured above, replaced the original ones there in 1911. Following the re-structuring of secondary education in Wirral, the school, now known as Henry Meoles, moved to its present site in Leasowe and Liscard Primary School now occupies the buildings pictured.

The board in the centre of this pair of large semi-detached houses seen in Manor Road in 1905, shows it was Wallasey High School for Girls. The school first opened on 10 September 1883 in the Liscard Concert Hall in Manor Road, with 4 teachers and 14 pupils. It transferred in September 1890 to the building above, which still stands at the junction of Stringhey Road, and is now called Manor Mansions. The fees for the girls, some of whom travelled from as far as Ellesmere Port and West Kirby, were in 1902 from £2.10.0. to £4.10.0. The school moved again in September 1909 to new buildings in Mount Pleasant Road and having survived a direct hit during World War II, it still flourishes today, although now called Weatherhead High School.

Mrs Drewe's shop on the right must have been a source of wonder to the children pictured, some of whom are bare-footed. Besides being a circulating library, newsagents, stationers, bookbinders and printers, it also sold fancy goods, postcards, dolls, toys, buckets and spades, and sweets. The shop, which was on the corner of Liscard Road and Liscard Village, was demolished not long after this photograph was taken in 1906. The Bank of Liverpool, now Barclays, opened on the site 22 August 1908. The two taller buildings beyond are still there today, as is the building in the distance on the corner of Manor Road, next door to which the Post Office opened in 1913.

A similar view to the one above but taken in the 1940's shows that the Bank of Liverpool has replaced Mrs Drewe's, and next door George Mason's van is parked outside his shop. The tower on the right in the middle distance is part of the fire station which opened on the corner of Manor Road in 1915. It was demolished in 1986 and the site is now a car park. A public shelter, known as the monkey house, once stood in the foreground. This was demolished in 1926 when public conveniences were built here. These were replaced by the roundabout, shown in the picture, which made way in turn for the new road lay-out in 1979. The Capitol Cinema on the left opened on 4 September 1926 and reopened after modernisation on 9 November 1959, closing on 23 February 1974. It is now a Bingo and Social Club.

This photograph was taken before 1913 when the Liscard Post Office, which had opened here at 226, Liscard Road about 1890, moved to new premises in Liscard Village. Next door, behind the handcart belonging to Davis & Sons, dyers and cleaners, is Tootle's pharmacy which catered for photographers and advertised its dark room for amateurs. Tootle marketed his own cures; Tootle's Bronchine for coughs, colds and asthma, etc; and Tootle's Pinol Creosote which, when inhaled from a handkerchief, cured coughs, colds, catarrh, etc; both items retailed at 1/– a bottle. This shop is now occupied by a driving school. The white building on the corner of Westminister Road was the North and South Wales Bank and is now a branch of the Midland. Charles Fry's pawnbroker's sign can be seen beyond the bank at 238-242 Liscard Road.

The N & S Wales Bank, seen on the right in Liscard Road on the corner of Westminister Road, in 1903, is the white building in the picture above and is now the Midland Bank. The Tower Hotel on the left is on the corner of Mill Lane, whilst the sign on the building behind the row of girls advertises the Queen's Hall – Gospel preachers every Sunday. The shop with the canopies, to the right of Mersey Coal Co's wagon, was Charles Fry's pawnbrokers shop, with sign above. In September 1911 Mr Fry exhibited the "Flaming Sun", an item of jewellery which he had bought at auction. It had belonged to Crippen's murdered wife and had also been worn by his girl friend, Ethel Neave. Large numbers of people were attracted here to view it.

This tramcar was lavishly decorated to celebrate the royal visit of King George V and Queen Mary on 25 March 1914 to lay the foundation stone of Wallasey's new Town Hall *(see page 28)*. Bunting and flags, together with 800 flowers, adorn the tram, whilst 2,300 light bulbs illuminate it. The King laid the foundation stone from Central Park by means of a cable connecting the switch to apparatus which controlled the lowering of the stone into position. Between thirty and forty thousand people attended and nine thousand schoolchildren had the pleasure of singing before the royal couple.

Taken in 1908, this country road is Mill Lane. Its two landmarks, Wallasey Water Tower and St. Alban's Roman Catholic Church, still survive today. The tower had a tank with a capacity of 150,000 gallons, and was built in 1860 as a distribution centre for water. It is now a listed building and houses a tyre depot. The foundation stone of St. Alban's Church was laid on 8 June 1852. The church opened 8 September 1853 and, in 1899, was completely renovated. Model Farm, built about 1845, once stood behind the wall on the left. This show farm of 440 acres attracted visitors from all parts of Europe, and the farmhouse still stands at the corner of Rullerton Road and Eldon Road.

Sir John Tobin, a Liverpool merchant, retired in the 1830's and took up residence in this building, which was then known as Moor Heys House. His son-in-law, Harold Littledale, later lived here. Following his death in 1889, the property, then known as Liscard Hall, was purchased by the Local Board. The house and grounds were then opened to the public. In 1900, at a cost of £2,000, the house was adapted for use as the School of Art. Adjoining land was later bought and the whole area, which now covers over 56 acres, became known as Central Park. The statue facing the School of Art in this 1906 picture was erected in memory of Wallasey men who lost their lives in the Boer War, 1899-1902.

This photograph was taken during 1916 or 1917 when Alderman Edwin Peace, pictured wearing his mayoral chain, was Mayor of Wallasey. He is posing in Central Park with the First Wallasey Boy Scout Troop whose official uniform was then grey shirts with red ties. Some of the scouts behind the mayor are sitting on the troop's hand-cart. A military band can be seen performing in the bandstand, possibly on an occasion which raised money for the war effort. Many ambitious galas were held here, one including a detachment of cavalry giving a realistic display of the relief of Mafeking. On another occasion a female parachutist descended from a balloon, missed the park and landed in the Great Float!

This picture taken in Poulton Road about 1906 shows a quiet meandering country lane, where cyclists have the road to themselves, and father is out pushing the pram. At this time Poulton was connected to Wallasey by narrow straggling highways. This peace was not to last long for, in 1909, land was purchased by the Corporation for road widening purposes in preparation for laying tram lines to connect Poulton with the other areas of Wallasey. Land to the right of this road was bought for this purpose, and the line opened 8 July 1910. Ivy Cottage, on the end at No. 433, Poulton Road, survived the development, but was demolished between the wars. Poulton cross roads are in the distance *(see below)*.

Taken from Breck Road in the same period as the previous photograph, the cottage pictured above can be seen straight ahead on the right side of Poulton Road. Mill Lane, with St. Luke's church on the corner, is off to the left, and beyond it is Poulton Hall. Erected at the end of the eighteenth century to replace the original seventeenth century building, the hall was demolished in 1933. Poulton Hall Road was then built on the site. Pool Inn, on the far corner of Poulton Bridge Road, is dated about 1880 and replaced the original seventeeth century building which stood lower down towards Wallasey Pool. The three cottages on the right have been demolished, but the tree still survives eighty years on.

Looking along Limekiln Lane about 1908, the house on the left which still stands on the corner of Poulton Bridge Road, is said to be the oldest surviving house in Wallasey, dating back to 1621. Known as Bird's House after its builder, a later generation built the barn to the left which was dated 1704. Molasses storage tanks now stand on that site. St. Luke's Church, in the background, was consecrated by the Bishop of Chester on 1 November 1900. It was built at a cost of £4,300 and had seating for 350. It replaced the original church building which had stood nearby and dated back to 1882. The buildings in front of the church have been demolished, and the site is now a car park. Balfour Road is now on the right.

The shops in Mill Lane, Poulton, which include a chandler, milliner, newsagent and confectioner, await custom. On the other side of Station Road, Mr. Edmondson poses in his white apron outside his grocers shop and to the left can be seen white gates which led to Liscard cum Poulton Station. Opened on the Seacombe branch of the Wirral Railway on 1 June 1895, it served the area until the last passenger service on 3 January 1960. The line was closed to goods traffic on 17 June 1963. The cutting at Poulton was widened and now takes the approach road to the Wallasey Road Tunnel under the Mersey, which was opened by Queen Elizabeth II on 24 June 1971.

This stone-built windmill, which was erected in 1765, stood on the Breck in Wallasey. It replaced an earlier mill which was shown on a map dated 1665. The villagers would buy their flour direct from the miller, and it was one of them who heard the sails break loose in a storm and probably saved the mill from burning down. The building became unsafe and was demolished in 1887. A Mr. George Peers built a house called Millthwaite on the site, and it was hoped to preserve some of the mill in the design, but this never happened. Millthwaite can be seen in the picture below.

THE BRECK, WALLASEY.   No 13

The Breck, part of which is pictured here, was formed from a sandstone ridge which extended along Claremont Road and on to Poulton Road. It was bought by Sir John Tobin in 1845 and worked as a quarry. Stone from here was used in the building of many of the local sandstone cottages, and it was also used in the building of Leasowe Road. The area is still an open space, and has been enjoyed by the children of many generations. The house in the background was Millthwaite, which replaced the old mill *(see previous picture)*. This house has subsequently been replaced by Millthwaite Court Flats in Millthwaite Close. St. Hilary's Church can be seen between the trees on the right.

Breck Road is named after the Breck which is situated to the right in an elevated position *(see previous picture).* The lady walking her spaniels is heading for the old schoolhouse. The early records of the school were destroyed in the fire of 1857 *(see page 48).* The original school was probably under the same roof as the church. It was moved in 1799 to the cottage pictured here which was in use until 1864 when, on January 19, the school was transferred to new buildings in St. Georges Road. A plaque on the well-preserved cottage relates its history to this day. The square walled enclosure beyond the lady seen here in 1910, was the Wallasey Pinfold, which has long since gone.

Taken from Church Hill, part of the Corononation Day procession on 22 June 1911 is seen proceeding along Claremont Road, Wallasey. The Mayor's Chaplain, the Rev. George Barber leads the first Mayor of Wallasey, J.J. Chester, followed by members of the Council. They are all heading for the celebration service at St. Hilary's Church. The landmarks on the left, beyond Belvidere Recreation ground, are St. Alban's Church spire and Liscard Water Tower, both in Mill Lane. The partly built houses pictured on the right are the rear view of numbers 3 to 13, Harrow Road. The site behind the crowd is now occupied by Uppingham Road and Radley Road.

Pictured here in 1915 is Wallasey Cottage Hospital at the junction of Claremont Road and Prospect Vale. Founded in 1866, its first premises, situated in Back Lane (now St. George's Road) in a building called Byron Lodge, opened in 1868 with only three beds. The foundation stone for the new building, with accommodation for twenty patients, was laid on 1 August 1885 by the Lord Bishop of Chester. An extension in May 1911 added a further nine beds, operating theatre, outpatients department and electric lift, at a total cost of £1,500. The hospital was further improved in 1920 and again in 1931, but, despite much local opposition, was closed on 8 August 1980 and the site sold for housing development.

Folly Lane once ran from Claremont Road behind the trams in this picture. It was a steep, narrow, cobbled path and followed the line of the church wall, continuing down to Wallasey Village. The extension of the tram systems from Mill Lane to Wallasey Village, which opened 7 February 1911, brought with it the widening of the top half of Folly Lane into what is now called Broadway. A row of whitewashed cottages once stood to the right of the children who are waiting for the tram. These cottages were demolished by 1913 when the site was enclosed by an extension to the church's boundary wall, which can be identified by the lighter coloured stones. The chickens roam free on the right, whilst the Parish Church stands proudly in the background.

The old Cheshire Cheese Inn pictured here was described in the 1830's as one of the largest buildings in the Village. The thatched tavern, with its tiny windows, worn steps and old sign attached to the chimney, ran from north to south. The out-of-character extension which ran up Church Hill, making it an L shaped building, can be seen on the far end of the building. The old inn, which had a road width of only six feet in front of it was demolished in 1885 and replaced with the present building. The thatched cottage on the right can be seen in the picture below.

A similar view to the picture above, but the old Cheshire Cheese Inn has been demolished and a new one built on a site further back. The whitewashed cottage with black timbers behind the horse and cart was a shop run by Mr. Jones. Beside the cottage a cow can be seen grazing in the garden, whilst an elegant carriage, with top-hatted driver, waits outside a shop at the top of School Lane. The large house on the hill, which stood overlooking the corner of St. Hilary Brow, was Wyncliffe, and is now No. 6, St. Hilary Drive, with Cliffe House and Breck Bank lower and to the right.

WALLASEY VILLAGE.

The only building surviving today in this 1913 view of Wallasey Village, taken from Breck Road, is the Old Cheshire Cheese Inn. This replaced the original inn which stood on a site in front of the present one *(see previous page)* and still has the 1885 date stone above the entrance pictured here. The horse and cart, which has two boys in the back with the milk churns, probably belonged to John Akrigg & Sons, dairymen, of 84, Wallasey Village. The building on the left, which was owned by John Nelson and the newsagent's and confectioner's shop next door, which was run by John Jones, were both demolished about 1921 when the road was widened. Church Hill, which is off to the right, can be seen in the next picture.

III. WALLASEY CHURCH DESTROYED BY FIRE 1857.

The congregation of St. Hilary's Church, Wallasey had complained for a long time about the cold church. So, in February 1857, the caretaker made a roaring fire which overheated the stove and set alight the church. The resulting burnt-out shell can be seen in this early photograph. Built in 1760, it was the fifth church to stand on this site, the first one dating back to Norman times. The Tudor tower, built in 1530, survived the fire and stands separate from the main church which was re-built in 1859. Stone from Rake Lane Quarry was used in the re-building.

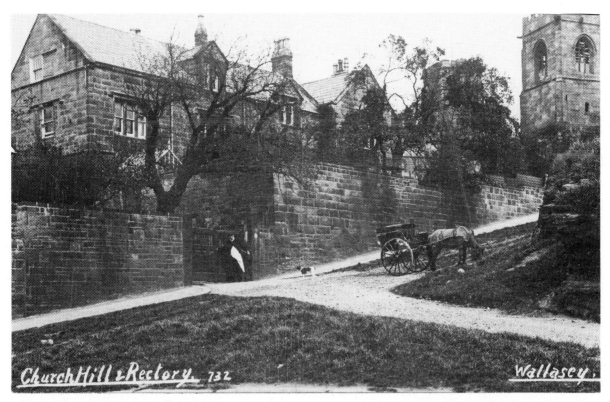

Mr. Abbott, the butcher, is about to make a delivery to The Rectory. His horse and cart are standing on the side of Church Hill. This building was erected in 1632 using material from the original Rectory. In 1695 it was extended and again in 1864, when a new wing was built using stone from Wallasey Old Hall which had just been demolished. The present Rectory was built on the site of, and using some stones from, Wallasey Old Hall and was first occupied in 1940. The former Rectory, which was burned down in the 1960's, was bought in 1981 and partly restored; a modern extension has been built on to the side of the old building.

Wallasey Village is hardly recognisable from this photograph of eighty years ago. On the right is Perrin Road and then a block of shops which includes Salisbury's greengrocers shop, whose cart is placed in the centre of the road in order to gain maximum publicity! The white building which juts out is the Black Horse Hotel. Dating back to 1722, it is believed to have taken its name from a horse entered in a race at Leasowe Racecourse. The hotel was demolished in 1931 when the road was widened and the new hotel built further back. The shops opposite, on the corner of Stonehouse Road, today number 75 to 79. The Parish Church Hall was built on land behind the wall on the left in 1906.

Wallasey Village is pictured about 1909 at the Leasowe Road junction, with St. John's Road off to the left. The block of shops on the left, which include the North and South Wales Bank, now the Midland Bank, stands on the site of buildings belonging to Lawton's farm. The thatched roof and tall chimneys belonging to the farmhouse can be seen behind the lamp and trough at the top of Leasowe Road. The road in the background was widened after the Black Horse Hotel was demolished in 1931 *(see previous picture)*. A milk cart stands outside an antique shop, whilst next door, a large sign in the shape of a brush draws attention to Hughes' Ironmongery.

As in the previous picture, this shows Leasowe Road at its junction with Wallasey Village. The lamp post pictured is still there but the trough has been removed. Lawton's thatched farmhouse has been demolished following a road-widening scheme in 1910, and a block of shops, including Roberts' the butcher on the left, stands on the site. The total length of Leasowe Road, including Reeds Lane, was widened at a cost of £135,000 following a proposal put forward in February 1921. The building behind the policeman was once Wallasey Reading Room which was closed in April 1900 due to poor attendance. One of the reasons for this was that smoking was not permitted in the public reading rooms!

This early photograph was probably taken about 1890, and shows a typical old Wallasey thatched cottage with a small upper room built under the high-pitched roof. It was said to have been occupied at one time by Edward Dodd, who was the village constable and stood in Wallasey Village near the junction with St. John's Road. The stone built cottage has its lower end windows blocked, probably to avoid paying window-tax. The cottage became a garage prior to the First World War and was demolished in the 1930's. Two ghostly figures can be seen in the road, caused by the subjects moving too quickly and making a blur on the photograph.

The Wesleyan Chapel in Wallasey Village, which opened in 1885 and seated 200, was vacated in 1910 when the congregation moved to new premises in Claremont Road. The former chapel then became the Wallasey Picturedrome and the sign can be seen above the gentleman to the right of the lamp post. It was opened 6 March 1911 under the management of Miss M. Hardy. Following the twice-nightly "beautifully clear" films, a Mr. Clutterbuck entertained the audience with appropriate pianoforte selections. He was replaced by a singer, Miss M. Solari, and later a comedian, Mr. Hal Rowe, also appeared. The cinema venture lasted less than a year. The building was then converted into shops which are now Nos. 131 to 137, Wallasey Village. Beechwood Avenue is to the right of the premises pictured.

The single storey shops which were originally the Wesleyan Chapel shown in the previous picture, can be seen directly behind the cyclist on the right in this 1930's view of Wallasey Village. The tallest building is still Nos 139 and 141, Wallasey Village, on the corner of Beechwood Avenue. The picturesque Willow Cottage on the left, which dated back to 1737, stood in the way of a road-widening scheme which was prepared by the Corporation as far back as 1906. It survived until March 1946, when its demolition was given the go-ahead by the Ministry. St. Mary's College was built on land to the left, the first phase of building being opened at Easter 1973.

The Cosmo Cinema pictured on the right in Wallasey Village, opposite Sandy Lane, was opened on 12 May 1913 and seated 700. It re-opened as the Coliseum Theatre on 24 June 1924 and, except for a brief period of two years when it became the Wallasey Picture House, continued as the Coliseum until it received a direct hit from a German bomb in March 1941, and was demolished soon afterwards. The Phoenix Cinema was opened on the site on 4 June 1951, and continued until the mid 1970's, when it was split into two mini-cinemas. However it closed on 6 July 1983.

The bunting is out as the Wallasey Silver Band leads the Wallasey Village Festival procession on 27 June 1910. Starting at St. George's School, they went along St. George's Road then through Wallasey Village, where they are seen here with the Wallasey Presbyterian Church in the background, ending up in a field near the Cottage Hospital in Claremont Road. On this annual event collections were made for local charities by using fishing nets on long poles or umbrellas inside out to catch the pennies. The lengthy programme of events which followed the parade included children dancing around the maypole, running races, tug of war and the greasy pole.

A similar view to that above, this shows Wallasey Village in the early part of this century before the area was developed. The gap between the buildings is Sandy Lane, the sign for which can be seen on the far wall. This row, know as Mason's Cottages, was bought by the Council for £2,000 prior to the widening of Sandy Lane, to make way for the new tram route from Mill Lane. This came to Wallasey Village via Claremount Road, Broadway, St. George's Road and Sandy Lane. In the picture above, taken June 1910, half of Mason's Cottages have been demolished; the rest were pulled down and the road widened in time for the route to be opened on 7 February 1911.

This peaceful scene taken in 1907 in Wallasey Village was soon to change. The opening in 1901 of Harrison Drive, which can be seen in the background, had increased the popularity of Wallasey shore. By the time Wallasey Village had been widened to take the double tram track, which came into operation 7 February 1911, the developers had already moved in, building shops, banks, cafes, etc. The buildings on the left behind the family group were replaced by shops. Green Lane is on the left of the horse and cart and the block of shops beyond are still there today. The cottages on the right were demolished in 1966 and the area now forms part of the site of the new Lighthouse Inn. They can be seen in the picture below.

Taken in Wallasey Village in the 1930's, the old Lighthouse Inn can be seen on the left. It was first licensed about 1860, although the building dates back a further hundred years, when it was originally two cottages. The beerhouse, together with three adjoining cottages and one acre of land at the rear, was bought by Birkenhead Brewery Company in March 1900 for £3,340. It had belonged to the estates of the late Sarah Kendrick who had owned it for 35 years. The four buildings to the right of the inn were demolished in April 1966, and the present Lighthouse Inn was erected on the site. The old inn was then demolished. The spire of the Presbyterian Church is in the background.

This photograph, looking along Wallasey Village from Harrison Drive, was taken prior to the First World War. The Bank of Liverpool, seen on the right at the corner of Groveland Road, was opened 15 November 1909. Today it is a branch of Barclay's Bank. The Grove Hotel, viewed on the left at the junction with Grove Road, advertises breakfasts, luncheons, and teas; upstairs became the Melody Inn Club in the 1950's, and was burnt down in the 1960's. The site of the hotel is now an open space. Beyond the hotel are three shops, including the Criterion which is still in business under that name. The block was extended and, by 1915, reached as far as the next shop pictured here on the corner of Sandiways Road.

HARRISON DRIVE, WALLASEY

The popularity of Wallasey shore when this early 1920's photograph was taken can be seen by the steady stream of people making their way down Harrison Drive. The cobbles on the left are in Groveland Road. Beyond the white gate which leads to the station, is the stationmaster's house, Station Cottage; its garden now forms part of the pavement. Windsors' Garage was built behind the tree on the left, and their showrooms were erected much later on the site of the cottage opposite. The tram lines on the right, which lead into Grove Road, were on the Mill Lane to Wallasey Village and Grove Road route which opened 7 February 1911.

Windsors' Grange Garage is pictured in Grove Road, Wallasey, about 1923. The building on the left, known as Grange Cottage, was owned in 1914 by Samuel Windsor, who was described then as a cow keeper. To the left of the cottage was Sandcliffe Road, having changed its name from Jockey Lane in the early part of this century. The garage was built by Samuel's widow, Mrs M.E. Windsor, in 1922. Shortly after, she built another garage in Harrison Drive *(see picture below)*. The Grove Road garage was sold about 1950 to Armstrong's Taxis, who ceased the engineering side of the business but continued selling petrol. There is still a garage on the site today, operated by Texaco.

Land owned by the railway in Harrison Drive was bought in the early 1920's by Mrs M.E. Windsor and the garage, seen here in 1926, was built to augment the one pictured above. In an advert of 1927 Windsors were described as sole agents in the area for the new Overland Whippet Saloon which cost £220. In 1934 the building was given a new facia which survived the damage caused by a bomb falling at the back of the garage on 22 December 1940. During the war the ground floor was commandeered by the National Fire Service and upstairs Reynolds manufactured tarpaulins. In 1955 a new single storey showroom was built adjoining the garage and the present showroom opposite opened in 1965. Windsors are today Wirral's leading Austin Rover dealer with over 64 years experience.

This 1912 photograph of Claremount Road, Wallasey is viewed from Grove Road. Prior to 1906, Claremount Road, formerly Top Lane, which was then still a narrow lane, ended at the top corner of the open ground pictured, which was known as Flynn's Piece. Access to Grove Road was then by footpath along the line of the road pictured or diagonally across Flynn's Piece which came out opposite Jockey Lane (now Sandcliffe Road). However, in April 1906 Mr. Lawrence Connolly offered to sell seven hundred square yards of land to the Council, which would enable the two roads to be joined. Mr. Connolly paid the cost of making the East side of the road, and the Council paid for the other half on the side of Flynn's Piece. This is still an open space today.

This Edwardian view of St. George's Road, when it was a country lane, was to change drastically when trams came to Wallasey Village in 1911. A directory of 1891 refers to Back Lane, but by January 1900, when several loads of cinders were put down to make the road less of a quagmire, it was know as St. George's Road – formerly Back Lane. In February 1906 it was described as a disgrace to the district but, as it was a private road, the Council had been unable to repair it. Later that year, due to heavy rains, the road was likened to a swamp with mud several inches deep. The Council later adopted the road and widened it sufficiently to take the double tram-tracks, the route opening on 7 February 1911.

(5) HARRISON DRIVE WALLASEY

Prior to 1900 there was no proper road access to the beach from Wallasey Village and, in December 1899, the Wallasey Council agreed to borrow £7,580 to construct a new road from Wallasey Village to the sea-shore. The old roadway was built up and in places was ten foot higher than the surrounding land. Even this did not stop the road being covered by sand blown from the sandhills. The new road was called Harrison Drive and was opened on 24 June 1901. It was used by locals and also trippers who came by train and, after February 1911, by tram.

The crowd has gathered around the sand model in Wallasey in the Autumn of 1914. This fine sculpture of a horse and soldier reflects the feelings of the day in the caption "His last farewell – Pals". The Great War had just started and initiated by Lord Derby, "Pals" battalions were formed locally, comprised of men from similar occupations. The Wallasey Sands were also perfect for motor-cycle races. The Chester Motor Club organised races on the sands at Harrison Drive and, in May 1932, a shore record was established on a Douglas Motor Cycle at 89.45 m.p.h.

The Harrison Drive Baths, pictured here, cost £35,000 and were opened on 8 June 1932 by Lord Derby and were hence called Derby Baths. These baths were opened two years before the famous New Brighton bathing pool and were frequented by local residents, whereas the New Brighton Baths were more popular with visitors. The verandah roof, pictured on the left, with the cafe overlooking the pool in the centre, could accommodate two hundred sunbathers. The pool, which had facilities for one thousand bathers, was a hundred yards long, twenty five yards wide and up to seven feet deep, with a capacity of 800,000 gallons of filtered sea water.

The 103rd Cheshire Home Guard Anti-Aircraft Battery was formed in 1942 to take over from the regulars. Men from Wallasey were invited to form one of the new "Z" rocket batteries. As the men operated part-time on a rota system, up to 1,600 men and 40 officers were recruited. The nine acre site allocated to the battery lay off Wallasey Promenade at the bottom of Sandcliffe Road; the houses on the right are in Warren Drive. The No. 6 Mark I (twenty barrel) projector, pictured here, was one of six allocated to Wallasey in June 1944. This was one of only six sites in Great Britain so equipped. The Battery was dismantled in December 1944.

Beyond the Harrison Park Sandhills, pictured in 1911, are the New Brighton Golf Links. This 9 hole golf club was founded in 1890 on 30 acres of land which had been farmed by a Mr. Cowdock, who lived in the small cottage pictured centre right. By 1911 the cottage was for the use of lady members. In 1910 the Council purchased the links for £15,750, and it became the first municipal golf club in the area. In December 1932 it was decided to extend the links to 18 holes at a cost of £1,500, which took three months to complete. The spire of New Brighton Presbyterian Church, opened in Ennerdale Road in July 1910 and New Brighton Tower can be seen in the background.

Wallasey Golf Club was formed in 1891 by some members of the Royal Liverpool Golf Club who found the Hoylake course to be overcrowded. The links were opened for play on 29 October 1891 and the clubhouse, which opened on Christmas Eve 1892, is pictured here c1906. Access to the club in these early days must have been a problem as the only approach was via Groveland Road and then across a sea of sand. In 1901 six hundred railway sleepers were laid as a path from Groveland Road along what is now Newport Avenue to the clubhouse. The Council purchased the Harrison Sandhills Estate in February 1922. The estate included the links, the acreage of which had to be reduced, but not the clubhouse. The ladies' pavilion was opened in September 1930 having been built at a cost of £600.

St. Nicholas' Church and the vicarage on the left in Groveland Road are viewed here from Bayswater Road. The church was built by the Harrison family in memory of their well-known parents, James and Jane Harrison, hence the church is also known as the Harrison Memorial Church. The foundation stone was laid by the Harrisons on 26 April 1910. Built of Storeton stone by J. Thomas of Oxton at a cost of £15,000, it seats up to 700. It was dedicated on 29 November 1911. The Harrison Memorial Hall, the foundation stone for which was laid on 21 May 1932 on a site next to the present Windsors' showroom in Harrison Drive, boasted a stage and seating for 500.

Taken from in front of the railway bridge in Leasowe Road in 1911, this picture shows the shops in Wallasey Village in the distance. The group on the left pose for the photographer by Probyn Road, whilst on the right there is no pavement and the only building is that of Spragg's Vale Brewery, which was established 1830-1840. By 1910 they operated three public and two fully licensed houses in Wallasey Borough, but in 1920 they were taken over by Higson's Brewery. The brewery building pictured, together with other properties and land in Leasowe Road, was bought by Wallasey Council under a compulsory purchase order in 1921. The total three mile length of Reeds Lane and Leasowe Road was then widened at a cost of £135,000.

Leasowe Castle, once known as Mockbegger Hall, is pictured here after it had been bought for £11,750 and converted into a convalescent home for railway workers which opened 12 June 1911. The central tower was constructed in 1593 by the Earl of Derby and was probably used for hunting purposes. By the late 17th century the castle was in a poor state of repair. It was acquired in 1802 by Mrs Boode and passed, on her death, to her son-in-law, Edward Cust, who repaired and extended it. On his death in 1878 the castle passed to the family and was sold in 1895, when it became an hotel before conversion to the convalescent home. It was purchased by Wallasey Corporation in 1970 and then, in July 1980, a local businessman converted the building into an hotel.

This old oaken seat, which once stood facing the sea in the grounds of Leasowe Castle, was known as Canute's Chair. The inscription seen carved into the wood, "Sea come not hither nor wet the sole of my foot", is traditionally attributed to that king. The chair is depicted in an old engraving of the Castle in Ormerod's History of Cheshire (2nd edition 1882) and was probably erected by Edward Cust *(see above)*. Although above the high-water line, it suffered from the weather and, before being repaired in 1912, was described as being in a dilapidated condition. It again fell into disrepair after the Second World War and was never restored.

Taken from the top of Leasowe Lighthouse *(see page 64)*, this was the view in the summer of 1911, with Wallasey in the background on the left. Bankfield House is in the foreground surrounded by tents and wooden holiday homes, whilst in the field beyond the Seabank Farm sports are taking place. The events included a ladies potato race, a slow bicycle race and pillow fights on a greasy pole. Behind this field, and running from right to left, can be seen the rear of houses in Pasture Road. Because of the weather campers only used this site from May to September. The population of Moreton, including Leasowe, was then 989, but was soon to increase dramatically *(see below)*.

This photograph, which was taken in the early 1920's, is of the same farm and fields pictured above but somewhat changed! Aptly entitled Bungalow Town, it shows how the population had increased from 989 in 1911 to 4,029 in 1921. The reason people moved and set up home here was the general housing shortage coupled with the area being unrated. All this conglomeration of caravans and huts, converted tramcars and railway carriages, had to be raised clear of the low lying ground because of flooding. Due to lack of adequate sanitation and water supply, the ditches were described as a collection of open sewers containing slime. By April 1928, when the Parish of Moreton became part of Wallasey, there were more than 2,000 insanitary dwellings.

This Venice of Wirral scene was a familiar one in the rainy months at Leasowe, when the only means of access was by boat, raft or duck-boards. The dwellings in the background are all raised clear of the water. Although conditions in these huts and caravans were described by sanitary inspectors as being far worse than city slums, Leasowe's health figures compared favourably with the rest of Wallasey. Immediately Wallasey Council became responsible for Leasowe in 1928 work was put in hand to improve sanitary conditions, build roads, remove insanitary dwellings and build new houses. By the outbreak of war in 1939 some 1470 dwellings had been removed and most of the problem dealt with.

Leasowe Lighthouse is seen on a postcard entitled "Canvas City", Leasowe 1907. By 1763 there were two lighthouses here. One suffered from sea damage and was replaced by that on Bidston Hill in 1771, whilst the present one bears the 1763 date stone. The last lighthouse keeper was Mrs Williams who took over the job from her husband and worked until the light was finally extinguished in 1908. She then moved into a nearby cottage and opened a tearoom on the second floor of the lighthouse. Wallasey Corporation purchased the building from Mersey Docks and Harbour Board for £900 in March 1930, but the doors have remained closed since Mrs Williams died in 1935.